NATIONAL GEOGRAPHIC

D0503808

Chores

Nick Bruce

◇ ◇ ◇ ◇ ◇ ◇ ◇ ◇ ◇

On **Monday** I sweep the floor.

On Tuesday I clean my room.

On Wednesday I set the table.

On Thursday I water the plants.

On Friday I empty the trash.

On Saturday my mom gives me money for doing my chores.

I save the money in my money box.